SAINT NICHOLAS
the Giftgiver

Retold & Illustrated by
NED BUSTARD

IVP
Kids

This book
is dedicated to
my sweet daughters
(*after all, I first wrote
this book for them*) and
to all of the children who
are yet to believe. —N. B.

InterVarsity Press • P.O. Box 1400, Downers Grove, IL 60515-1426 • ivpress.com • email@ivpress.com

Text and Illustrations ©2021 by Ned Bustard

All rights reserved. No part of this book may be reproduced in any form without written permission from InterVarsity Press. InterVarsity Press® is the book-publishing division of InterVarsity Christian Fellowship/USA®, a movement of students and faculty active on campus at hundreds of universities, colleges, and schools of nursing in the United States of America, and a member movement of the International Fellowship of Evangelical Students. For information about local and regional activities, visit intervarsity.org.

Scripture quotations are from the New Revised Standard Version Bible, copyright © 1989 National Council of the Churches of Christ in the United States of America. Used by permission. All rights reserved worldwide.

ISBN 978-1-5140-0180-6 *(print)* • ISBN 978-1-5140-0181-3 *(digital)*

Printed in China

Library of Congress Cataloging-in-Publication Data

A catalog record for this book is available from the Library of Congress.

P	18	17	16	15	14	13	12	11	10	9	8	7	6	5	4	3	2	1
Y	36	35	34	33	32	31	30	29	28	27	26	25	24	23	22	21

On the night before Christmas,
so the old stories say,
Saint Nicholas rides
in a magical sleigh.
But what is the truth,
and what are the legends?
Who is this giftgiver,
and why all the presents?

The stories all begin
in the land of Turkey,
where Nicholas was born,
making a family of three.
He was baptized and loved,
but before he was grown
his parents both died,
leaving Nick all alone.

So Nicholas lived
with his uncle and grew
to love our dear Savior,
who makes all things new.
That Savior is Jesus,
God's very own Son,
a stable-born King—
the true Risen One!

While still a young man,
Nick sailed off to see
the blest Holy Lands
all around Galilee.
Near there he lived
in a cave for his house,
he prayed all alone
(save for a wee mouse).

Soon a very bad king,
Diocletian, arose.
He made faith illegal—
jailing Nick and all those
who said they loved Jesus
—in each country and state.
But then they were freed
by Constantine the Great.

So Nick settled in Myra
once he was free
and taught folks the Bible
down by the sea.
In that bustling town
Nick helped one and all
—any person in need:
young, old, short, and tall.

And then in Nicaea,
amidst hot debate,
a lie about Jesus
Arius did state.
Nick would not sit by
and let falsehoods increase,
so he did all he could
to stop that bad priest.

Nick cared for the church,
serving as their bishop:
he shared with God's people
both the Word and the Cup.
And in thanks for grace
from God the Almighty,
he gave gifts to the weak,
the sick, and the needy.

He showed great kindness
to a poor family
by aiding three sisters
faced with calamity.
On one very dark night
Nick snuck into the cold
and toss'd through their windows
three bags filled with gold.

Through the years Nick grew
a little round belly
that shook when he laughed
(like a bowl full of jelly).
Folks say that he died in
three hundred forty-three,
on December the sixth
. . . well-loved and godly.

But SOME stories say
that on Christmas Eve
Nick carries a sack with
gifts, treasures, and treats.
For him time has stopped
in some curious way—
the hands of the clock
forever delayed.

Like the Wise Men who brought
good gifts to bestow,
there's no length to which
Saint Nick will not go—
he tucks gifts in stockings
by chimneys with ease,
or nestles them under
bright evergreen trees.

On and on through the night,
though cold, he is merry.
His cheeks are like roses,
his nose like a cherry!
And whenever he's ready,
a small sleigh will appear,
spangled over with bells
and drawn by reindeer.

Nick gave the deer names
like Blitzen and Dasher,
fast as comets they soar—
sometimes even *faster*!
They say that by magic
o'er the housetops they fly,
with a sleigh full of gifts
across the night sky.

Saint Nicholas follows
our Giftgiver above
and gives to show others
God's wonderful love.
He'll deliver delights
until Jesus descends—
for Saint Nick it will stay
Christmas Eve 'til the end.

A NOTE FROM THE AUTHOR

The earliest accounts of Nicholas's life were recorded after his death, so little can be known about him with much certainty. Historians generally agree that Nicholas was born on March 15, 270, in Patara, Turkey, to a wealthy Christian couple, and that they both died while Nicholas was still young, leaving him to be raised by his uncle who was an abbot. While still in his early thirties Nicholas was ordained a bishop, but was then jailed during the Great Persecution. Soon after his release, Nicholas was sent to the Council of Nicaea where a priest named Arius claimed that Jesus was not equal to God the Father. This so upset Nicholas that he slapped Arius in the face!

Many legends grew around Nicholas over the centuries, the most famous being the story of how he secretly gave bags of gold to a poor man's daughters so the young women could be married. Some of his other good works include freeing innocent soldiers from the gallows, saving sailors during a storm, and rescuing children from a barrel of pickling brine. Even more fantastic stories came later, such as Nicholas finding a husband for a mouse, feeding a widow using only three magic fish, and being drawn through the sky in a sleigh pulled by magic reindeer.

What's interesting is that both history and legend portray for us a man moved to action by his faith. The apostle John wrote that we love because God—the *greatest* Giftgiver—first loved us. And it was God's generous love that filled Nicholas with gratitude, prompting him to respond with love and generosity to others.

After you've read *Saint Nicholas the Giftgiver,* you might want to think about these two questions and share your responses with one another:

What's the greatest gift you've ever given?
What's the greatest gift you've ever received?

May you experience joy and wonder
at Christmas and all year long!

...Ned

Every generous act of giving, with every perfect gift, is from above, coming down from the Father of lights, with whom there is no variation or shadow due to change. JAMES 1:17 (NRSV)

If you want a more in-depth study of Saint Nicholas, some recommended books include: *The Saint Who Would Be Santa Claus: The True Life and Trials of Nicholas of Myra* by Adam C. English, *The Real St. Nicholas: Tales of Generosity and Hope from Around the World* by Louise Carus, and *The True Saint Nicholas: Why He Matters to Christmas* by William J. Bennett.